Contents

Any words appearing in the text in bold, **like this**, are explained in the glossary.

What is a report?

A report is a piece of writing that describes the 'what, how and why' of something that has happened. There are many different types of report but they all include three important features:

- clear explanation and description of the subject
- **research** and facts about the subject
- personal comment or **opinion**.

Types of report

A report can be as simple as a diary entry. It can also be about an **issue** (such as wearing school uniform) or about a piece of school work (like a science project you have done). Other types of report include **articles** in newspapers and magazines, which can tell the story of an event in the news. A **review** tells the reader about a book, film or event and gives them a personal opinion. A **recount** tells readers about an event.

How do I go about writing a report?

There are some basic steps you need to follow to write a report:

- **Make a plan**
  Decide how you will arrange your information. Think about what to include at the start of the report, how you develop it and how you end it.

- **Do some research**
  Research can be watching something happen, or finding information in books or searching on the Internet. It can also involve interviewing people to find out their opinions.

- **Think about your research**
  You have to **analyse** your research, which means you have to think about the facts and work out what they mean.

- **Think about who will read it**
  Your readers will affect the way you write your report. If it is for a school magazine, make the writing sound chatty and

friendly. If it is to be read by people you don't know in a local newspaper, you will want to make it sound more **formal**.

- **Write it clearly**
  Write your report in a clear way, so your reader can understand and enjoy it.

- **Make it look right**
  Lay out everything about the subject neatly and clearly. Keep the reader interested by breaking up your writing with headings, lists and separate sections.

- **Have an opinion**
  Give an opinion or some advice about the subject. This comes in the last section of your report.

@ Activity – reading reports

Read some different types of reports, for example reviews of music or computer games, book reviews in newspapers, perhaps your school magazine. Try to explain the differences between them all. Why was each one written and who for?

Think about the different reports and ask yourself these questions:
- How long is the report you are reading?
- How does the report 'sound'? Is it friendly and chatty or business-like and formal?
- Do you think it is clear and easy to read?
- What does the writer think about the subject?
- How does the report end?

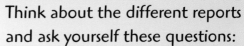

'The review says this film is as exciting as watching paint dry!'

Make a plan

You need to organize the information you will put in your report. A report should be written in clear steps and be easy to understand. If you plan your report well it will make writing it easier.

Break it up

Try making a rough plan for your report. You will need to start with an introduction. Next you might have some **background information** telling readers about the subject. Then write the main part of your report, including interesting points. Finally, give your own views and thoughts in a **conclusion**.

Think about the order you will put things in. Divide your information into sections, each with a heading. You can then write brief notes about what you will include under each heading. Your notes might look like this plan here.

A report on school sports day

Introduction
• Explain that the report is about sports day that happens every year

Background on sports day
• Where it is held
• Why it is held
• Who goes to it

Details of the races
• What races were held
• Who took part
• Who won

Conclusion
• Do people like sports day?
• What could be better about it

Top tip

Although your plan does not need to list everything you will say in your report, make sure it covers the important facts. When you come to write the report you can add in little descriptions to give readers a 'picture' of what sports day was like, for example. Put these anywhere where you think they fit.

Activity – proper planning

At some point in their time at school, everyone reads a play by William Shakespeare. He is the greatest playwright who ever lived! There are thousands of books, **articles** and even films about his works, but we don't know much about his private life.

Imagine you are going to write a report on Shakespeare's life. Write a plan of what information you would like to include. You might write about where he was born, where he lived and how old he was when he died. You can mention his plays but don't say too much about them – remember your report is about his life.

Your plan should show what order you would put your information in. There is no need to write too much, just note down the important points.

William Shakespeare – what did he do when he wasn't writing plays?

Fact finding

You need to include facts in your reports to explain and support any **opinions** you give. How do you find these facts? By doing **research**. Research can involve interviewing people or collecting facts from books or the Internet. It can also mean visiting places or watching an event.

Before you start:
- know roughly what you need to find out for each section of your report
- think about where to look and who to ask
- be open to surprises. Try not to make up your mind about something before you do research.

Find out what people think

Imagine you are writing a report of a school trip to an outdoor activity centre. You will need to interview some people who went on the trip to get their opinions. Talk to your classmates and teacher. Ask them what their favourite activity was. Did they enjoy the trip? If so, why? If not, why not?

Top tip

Prepare questions, but let people offer their own ideas as well. Ask them what they think. They might tell you something you never thought about asking!

Where to look

For some reports you need to look for facts in books or on the Internet. Make a note of where you might find things. For example, jot down possible search words to find websites on your subject. Don't start reading websites that are not important to your report. When you do find useful facts, make clear notes.

Here are a few rules for good note writing:
- Make sure you understand what you are reading.
- Be brief, but get all the facts you need.
- Make sure you copy **quotes** word for word.
- Keep control of your notes. File them!

Activity – research, research, research

Imagine you are writing a report called 'School uniforms: good or bad?' for your school newsletter.

Do some research for the report:

1 Find out what everyone is supposed to wear. Look in your school handbook to see what it says.
2 Does everyone wear the uniform? What happens if they don't?
3 What does your class teacher think about school uniforms? Try to sum up what he or she says in a few lines.
4 Prepare four or five questions to ask three people in your class. For example, 'Do you like the school uniform?', 'Do you think all uniforms should be got rid of?', 'Should the uniform be changed?'. Try to sum up and write down their views in a few lines, too.
5 Find out what your parents or guardian think about school uniforms. Do they think that it is good for you to have to wear a uniform? Why?
6 If you can, find out if people from other schools like having a school uniform.

Working things out

The proper word for thinking about information in reports is **analysis**. This means studying the information that you have discovered through your **research**. You need to work out what the information means and how it fits together so you can come to a **conclusion**.

Detective work

Analysis is a bit like detective work. Take note of what is important and leave out things that don't fit your report. If you have done a lot of research you need to know where to start:

- Make a list of all the information you have. Cross out the things that don't fit the point of your report.
- Decide what are facts and what are people's personal ideas.
- If there are two sides to an argument, make 'for' and 'against' lists.
- Think about the reasons behind people's views. For example, some people might support a plan to build a new shopping centre because they want to buy and run shops there.

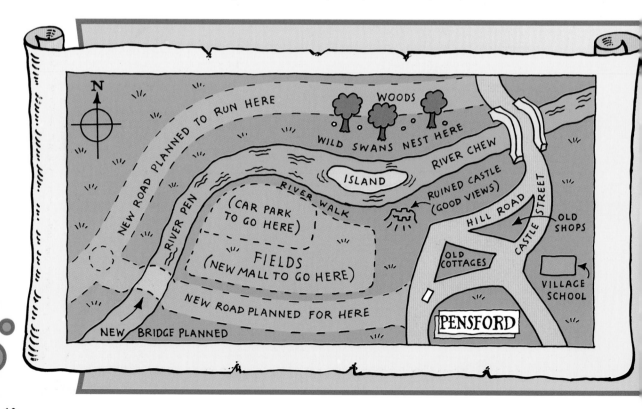

Top tip

You might change your views about a subject after you have looked at all the facts. Be open to this. If you do change your views, explain why in your report.

Activity – Pensford town

Look at the map of Pensford, a historic country town. There is a plan to build a new road along the riverbank and a shopping centre on the meadows. Some people want this to happen. Others do not, and have formed a **protest** group to keep Pensford as it is.

Read the two sides of the argument below and analyse the facts. Use them to write a paragraph saying whether or not you think the plan should go ahead.

For the plan
- Traffic is terrible in Castle Street.
- Heavy lorries go past the school and are damaging old buildings.
- People go elsewhere to shop because they cannot park.
- Only local people use the walk along the river.
- The road will take traffic out of the town centre.
- New shops will bring people and money to the town.
- Jobs will be created.
- If the shops are not built here they will be somewhere else and Pensford will lose out.

Against the plan
- Children play by the riverbank.
- The town's character will be destroyed by a new road.
- Apart from shops, the plan will not bring anything useful to the town (no new leisure centre for a start).
- Most people in Pensford have cars and are happy to shop in towns nearby.
- New shops will bring more traffic and traffic fumes into the area and will harm wildlife.

Remember the reader

Most reports are written for other people to read. These people are called your **audience**. You have to match the report to the group of people who will read it. Before you start writing your report, think about these things:

- **What do you need to include?**
  If people know a lot about the subject, you don't have to include as much **background information**. For example, if you are writing a report about your school for students then you don't have to describe basic things about the school. However, if you are writing for a national magazine you will need to include more facts, such as where your school is.

- **What does your audience expect?**
  People will expect your style of writing to match what the report is about. If you are writing a news report about an accident, your style will be serious or **formal**. For a **review** of a funny end-of-term play your style can be chatty and friendly (**informal**).

- **The tone of your report**
  The **tone** of your report is how you 'sound' to your audience. The tone is set by your choice of words and phrases. Different words can make your writing sound more or less chatty. You choose formal words and phrases to write a report on a visit to your school by a famous person:

  > We were delighted that Lady Sarah Ratcliff had time to visit the school. She had many encouraging things to say to us.

In a review of the latest computer game you might use the sort of words you say in conversation with your friends.

  > It's got fab graphics and loads of special features ...

When writing a report, stick to one style and tone throughout – don't try to mix them. Words like 'fab' and 'loads' would be odd in a formal report. Read your report through to check whether the words you have chosen are suitable.

Activity – writing for an audience

Think of something special you have done recently at school. Perhaps it was taking part in a sports match, a play or going on a trip.

Write a report for your school magazine. Your audience are the other pupils in the school. They will know some of the people involved and a bit about the event.

Describe:
- what the event was
- any special or funny things that happened
- what you learned.

Now write a report on the same subject for a group of inspectors who want to find out what happens at your school. They want a clear, serious and fact-filled report. They don't know anything about the people at your school.

MAG

SCHOOL

Year 5 go wild in the country!

Everyone gets their hands dirty on the farm

REPORT

A report on Year 5's visits to Newlands Farm

A practical environment project

Grab the reader's attention

Every report needs a strong introduction. You need to grab your reader's attention. You want them to understand and enjoy your report, so write clearly and accurately.

The right introduction

Plan and write your introduction carefully. Say clearly what the report is about and if necessary why it has been written. Include a sentence saying what sort of **conclusion** you come to at the end of the report.

Enjoy my report!

Even a report on something serious needs an introduction that makes readers feel they will enjoy reading it. Make the opening clear and short. For example, if you are writing about your favourite computer game, you could say:

> *'Danger garden' is a computer game that combines garden design with a 'hunt and destroy' game. You build a garden and then have to chase villains through it.*

Top tip

Your introduction should give the reader any **background information** they might need before reading the rest of the report. Remember that your readers will not always know what you are writing about.

Pace yourself

When you write the main part of the report, don't try to describe absolutely everything. Only include background information that is really needed for the report to make sense. However, make sure that you do include all the important details.

Write with style

Think about the sort of sentences you write. Don't use lots of short, sharp sentences, or long ones that go on and on. Aim for a mixture of different types, for example:

- Simple sentences, such as *Class four visited Bent Sticks farm.*
- Compound sentences, for example *The farm is a 'working farm' and also a centre that school parties can visit.*
- Complex sentences, like *Sheep, pigs and goats are kept in the barns when it is cold at night.*

Exclamations can make your writing sound more exciting: *There is also a huge bull called Harry!* But don't use too many or they will lose their effect.

Activity - make your interests interesting

Write the opening one or two paragraphs of a report describing something that interests you. It could, for example, be about a computer game or a band.

Write a fairly short, clear description of your subject. Imagine the reader has never heard of the band you love. What do you need to tell them in these first paragraphs so that they understand the rest of the report? Make sure the way you write makes them want to keep reading!

'Re-mix' are a chart topping band whose first hit 'I want to be with you' was Number One for six weeks ...

Manchester United is the most famous football team in England. Their home ground is Old Trafford.

The end of the report

How you finish a report is important. You need to write a clear **conclusion** and sum up your facts. You will also write most of your personal comments in the last section of your report.

The right ending

Different reports need different sorts of endings. For example:

- A report into an **issue** or 'problem' needs a conclusion that suggests what can be done to make things work. This can be a list of points and ideas. For example, a report on why a youth club is losing members might have the following suggestions:

> 1 Increase the opening hours at the weekend
> 2 Have all-girls or all-boys nights once a week
> 3 Install a pool table and a good music system.

- You could also end a report into a 'problem' by summarising the advantages and disadvantages of the different sides of the question or argument. Say what you think is the best thing to do.
- End a **review** by saying whether you liked what you have written about. Give clear reasons for your **opinion**.
- The conclusion for a science report will include the results of any experiments, and what they showed. There is no need for personal opinion.

Top tip

A reader should finish your report knowing more about the subject than before. Think about how much of your opinion or feelings you should include in your conclusion. Saying how something like a book or film made you feel might be just what the readers of a review want.

Activity – points of view

Some people say that television shows too many programmes that just entertain us. They think there are not enough serious programmes to educate people. Do you think this is true? Does it matter if TV just entertains you when you are tired after a hard day at school?

- Look at the television schedule for one afternoon after school (not cable or satellite), and watch a variety of programmes.
- Write a short report describing what you found. Say whether you think most of the programmes were 'easy entertainment'. Were there a few/some/a lot of programmes which made you think about important ideas?
- In your conclusion, make it clear what you think about the balance of programmes. Don't just describe what you saw.
- Now try to write another ending! This time give the opposite point of view.

Where I found my research

In reports where you have carried out **research** to find out information, you should list all your **sources**. These are books, **articles** or Internet sites where you found the information. Some readers might want to read these sources themselves.

Where do you list your sources?

At the end of the report you should add a section called an **appendix**. If you need more than one of these they are called appendices. For example, you could have separate appendices for books and Internet sites.

Number each appendix and give the following details:

- For books give the title, author, name of publisher and date:

> *Breakfast Foods, Jim Egg, Food Press, 2000*
>
> *Dentists of the World, Jemima Drill, Toothstone Publishing, 2001*

- For websites give the site name, for example, www.heinemann.co.uk.
- For articles give the title of the article, the author's name, the title of the magazine and the number – or month and year – of the issue.

Top tip

Think of interesting ways to display information. **Pie charts** and graphs can be quick and easy ways of showing facts, and make your reports look special.

Who I talked to

If you have interviewed people, you should say how many you interviewed, and where and when you did this. This information will be in a separate appendix. You might also have found out interesting extra information which does not fit into your report. This can be added to your appendix too.

@ Activity – travel facts

Interview everyone in your class about the way they get to school: by bus, train, car, bike, on foot – or even on roller blades! Make a graph or pie chart from the information you collect.

Now interview a selection of people. Ask them:

- Why do people use the bus? Do they like it? Are there problems with travelling by bus?
- Do people walk because they like it, or do they not have a choice?
- Do the cyclists feel safe on the road and happy leaving their bikes at school?
- Is coming by car the best and easiest way? What problems does it cause other people?

Think of interesting ways to display all this information in an appendix. This table shows one way:

Bus users

Total	Like the bus	Don't like the bus	No opinion
12	8	4	0

Walk to school

Total	Like the walk	Don't like the walk	No opinion
11	7	2	2

Make it look right

Reports need to look good because you want people to read them. Your report should be tidy, with all the information laid out clearly. Make your report look interesting by breaking it up into easy-to-read sections.

Space it out

Use paragraphs to break up your writing. Start a new paragraph every time you begin a new topic within your report.

You often need more than just paragraph breaks to make your report look clear. You could:

- start new sections with **sub-headings**, even if the sections are quite short
- make numbered lists
- use bullet points.

Lists can save words in long reports. Imagine you are writing a report about shopping in a town centre versus going to an out-of-town mall. You could divide your ideas into four neat lists: two on the advantages and disadvantages of town centre shopping, two on the advantages and disadvantages of the mall.

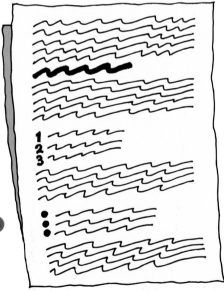

Word processing your report

If you have a computer at home or at school use it to write your reports. Word processing can make a report look very smart. You can use bold, italic, different **fonts** and colour to make sub-headings and lists show clearly. Experiment with the features on your computer to create tables and newspaper-style layouts. But be careful not to use too many different fonts and features or your report will look messy.

Top tip

Think about adding some pictures to your report. If you have created graphics like pie charts to back up your facts, you can paste them in too. Don't forget to tell your readers what the graphics or pictures are about, though! Use captions to do this.

Computer know-how

Here are a few hints for using the tools on your computer:

- Use the tab key to indent and line up your blocks of type.
- Use the electronic spellchecker to help check your spelling and grammar.
- If you have 'print preview' on your computer, check the position of the type on the page before you print.

Activity – special effects

Take any report you have written and type it on a computer. Lay it out clearly. Use some text effects (italic, bold, different fonts, colour) to make the report look attractive to read.

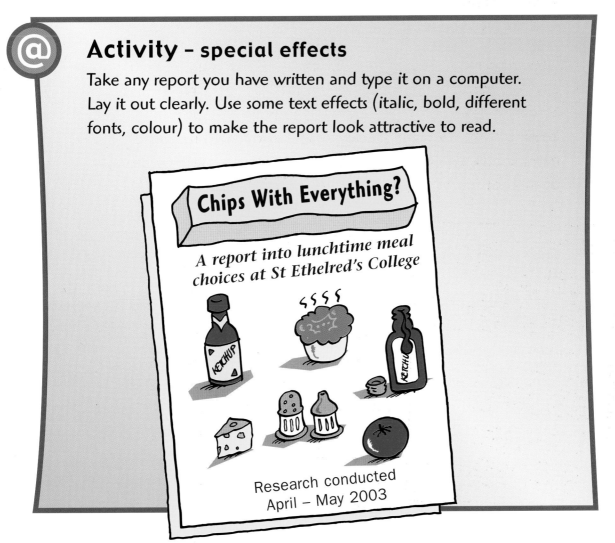

Reviews

Most people at school have to write **reviews** of books, plays or school trips. A review describes an event or a performance, and gives an **opinion** on it. Some reviews compare different products. For example, computer magazines review games from different manufacturers. They compare them to each other and say which is best.

Why do people read reviews?

People read reviews because they may want to know about something before they spend time or money on it. For example, they might want help to decide what film to go and see.

A film review must say what sort of film it is. Tell your readers a bit about it, bringing in things like:
- what the story is about
- where it is set
- who the characters are
- what sort of film it is (for example, comedy, action).

You might also bring in **background information** (like a bit of news about the film star appearing in it). You end by giving your opinion of the film.

Good reviews can help you decide which films to go to see.

Top tip

Be careful not to give too much away in your review. If you are writing about a book, for example, don't tell readers exactly how it ends!

Expressing opinions

When you give your opinion in a review make sure you:

- explain exactly what you are praising or criticizing
- say exactly why you think it was good or bad
- balance good and bad comments. Don't just say, 'It was rubbish!' – give reasons why you did not like it.

A good way of making clear whether or not you liked something is to end with a **recommendation**. For example:

> If you like a good adventure this is a good read, but if you prefer books that are more like 'real life', you will be disappointed. The events and characters aren't really believable, but the clever plot makes this book worth reading.

Activity – TV review

Choose a programme on television and watch it carefully.

Write a review of the programme. Begin by describing what it is. Imagine you are writing for someone who has never seen it.

Mention things you especially liked or disliked. Don't just describe the story, think about the acting and the choice of locations, where scenes were filmed.

Finish by saying whether you liked or disliked the programme overall, giving reasons for your opinions. Suggest the sort of person who might enjoy it.

Newspapers and magazines

Newspapers and magazines are full of **articles**. These are forms of reports. Articles have to capture the reader's interest and give a lot of information within a short space. You might write an article for your local paper about something that interests you. How do you do it?

Writing articles

Think about these points when you write an article:

- Make your opening sentence sound exciting. You want to grab the readers' attention when they are flicking through the pages:
  When people go to the museum they are in for a surprise.

- Bring in some **background information** to help the reader understand the subject:
  People have always loved dinosaurs. Now they can visit the museum to see their favourite – Tyrannosaurus Rex.

- Keep paragraphs short. Each paragraph should present no more than one or two clear points.

- Match your **tone** to the subject of the article. If it is a serious **issue** don't be jokey.

- If you interview people, quote only the most important things that they say:
  'I used to think that history was boring, but the Tyrannosaurus makes it really exciting!'

- How will you end your article? Use a really good **quote** from someone, or finish with your own **opinion** like you would in a **review**.

Top tip

Before you begin writing, make a note of the most interesting things about your subject. When you have finished, check that you have included all of them. Articles should be packed with interest and detail.

Activity – a personal account

Read the article that appeared in the *Bossetshire Times*. It is a very factual article. Now imagine you were one of the protesters from the village.

Write a more personal **recount** of the day for a local newspaper, saying what happened and why you are against the runway. What did it feel like to be sitting out on that runway?

–Bossetshire Times–
BT

Protesters sit on new runway!

Wildhall airport has opened its new runway. Bigger planes can use the airport, and many more flights are planned. A spokesperson said 'People all over Bossetshire will be able to fly to new destinations thanks to this new runway.'

But things have started badly. Villagers from Muckbury have been **protesting** against the runway which is close to their village. They are worried about noise and pollution, and of the danger of a crash. They say the peace of their village has been destroyed.

Fifty villagers – from elderly people to mothers with babies – broke through the airport security fence and staged a sit-in on the runway. Police were called, and three people were arrested for trying to paint 'NO MORE PLANES' on the runway. An incoming plane had to land at London's Heathrow airport instead.

Dear diary

When you write private diary entries in your own diary you are writing a personal type of report that is not for others to read. You describe things that have happened and how you feel. But some people write diary reports for other people to read.

Different diaries

Newspapers often run 'day in the life of' type **articles**. These are where a famous person describes their typical day. You could write a report like this on what happens during a term at school. Write the days and dates as **sub-headings** and describe one or two interesting things under each:

> 15 July
> Today was prize giving. Everyone was very excited because we got free food and had no lessons all afternoon.

In this type of diary, make sure you include important facts as well as your own thoughts. If you are writing about prize giving make sure you say who won what prize!

Top tip

Whether you are writing in your private diary or making a diary-type report for others, don't write about things that only really matter to you or it will become boring!

A research diary

Keeping a diary can help you find out about a subject. You could write diary entries about a nearby nature reserve. Visit it once a month and describe what you see. Over time your diary will show how the animals, trees and plants that live there adapt to the seasons. Use different sub-headings to make it clear.

> MARCH
> **Birds**
> The sparrows are collecting twigs for their nests.
> **Plants**
> Daffodils are out on the sunny bank, but on the shady side there are no flowers yet.

Activity – holiday heaven

What is your dream holiday? Where would you go? Imagine your dream has come true.

Write a brief description of what you imagine doing on the first day. (Don't forget to include who you went with!) Do this under the heading 'Monday'.

Do the same for the next six days of the week. Imagine all the things you see and do.

Finish by writing down how you imagine feeling at the end of the week.

The first time I saw the beach it was even better than I had imagined. The sand was so white, and the sea was deep, deep blue.

Polishing your report

Has your finished report done what it set out to do? Read it through carefully and use the following checklists to make sure your report is as good as it can be.

Structure

Does your report have:
- a good introduction to interest the reader?
- a main part divided into sections in a clear, logical way?
- sections in the right order? For example, if you are describing a day out, have you started with the morning and ended with the journey home?
- a strong ending, possibly including some personal **opinion**?

Style and subject

Have you checked that:
- your report has a clear style, and a nice mix of different types of sentences?
- the **tone** (chatty or **formal**) is right for the people who will read it?
- the style and tone are the same throughout the report?
- there is enough **background information** for readers to understand what you are writing about?
- the report includes all the important information?
- the report does not include unimportant facts?

Layout and presentation

Have you made sure that:
- the report looks neat?
- you have used **sub-headings** to start sections?
- you have used bullet points and lists to break up long paragraphs?
- your information has been turned into graphs, charts or tables in an **appendix** if necessary?
- your spelling, grammar and punctuation are accurate?

Reviews and articles

Here are some points to consider when writing **reviews** or **articles**.

For reviews, make sure you:
- describe what you are reviewing at the start
- concentrate on things you particularly liked or disliked
- end with a **recommendation**, for example: *Go and see this film!*

For newspaper or magazine articles, make sure you:
- make your opening sentence interesting to grab the readers' attention
- include **key facts** and detail
- say as much as you can with as few words as possible.

Activity - report writer

There are plans to turn an old school near you into a youth club. The council asked a group of young people to write a report on the sort of club people might want. They've got stuck, and have asked you to help them, because you are a well-known expert writer of reports!

Write a short set of notes to them saying:
- how they should plan their **research** (who to talk to)
- what sections they might need in their report (what things the council want to know)
- what sort of **conclusion** you have come to (give the council some recommendations).

Glossary

analysis looking at the facts and working out what they mean

appendix a separate section added to the end of a report giving extra information other than in the main text, such as a list and tables. If you have more than one appendix they are known as appendices.

article report in a newspaper or magazine

audience particular group of people that a report is written for

background information facts and details that are important to help a reader understand a report or review

conclusion end of a report. In some reports, this is where you give personal views and thoughts about the subject and sum up the report as a whole.

font style of letters that are a particular shape. A computer usually has lots you can choose from. Times New Roman and Arial are the most well known.

formal (writing) opposite of chatty, friendly writing. Formal writing style is often used in serious reports.

informal (writing) chatty, friendly writing that you would use in reports written for friends or your school

issue a matter or subject that is being talked or written about

key facts most important facts in a report or review

opinion personal feelings on a subject

pie chart way of displaying information in segments in a circle (like slices of a round pie)

protest to show disagreement with a law, idea or event

quote repeat exactly what someone has said

recommendation clear piece of advice given at the end of a report

recount report telling the reader about an event or a series of events

research process of finding out information

review an article giving a personal opinion to the reader about a book, film or event

sources places where you find out information, usually books and magazines

sub-heading or **sub-head** small titles inserted at the start of sections within a report, or between paragraphs in a review

tone how a report sounds (for example friendly or business-like)

Find out more

Here are some books to enjoy. You might find ideas in them for your own writing.

Behind Media: Newspapers, Catherine Chambers (Heinemann Library, 2001). Looks at the people and processes involved in making a newspaper, including gathering news and writing articles.

The Secret Diary of Adrian Mole Aged 13³/₄, Sue Townsend (Penguin, 2002). Imaginative diary entries of a teenage boy.

Index